FACTS AND FICTION ABOUT DRUGS™

OPIOIDS

KERRY BENSON

rosen publishing's
rosen
central®

New York

To William Benson Jr., who lost his life to the opioid crisis in 2010

Published in 2020 by The Rosen Publishing Group, Inc.
29 East 21st Street, New York, NY 10010

Copyright © 2020 by The Rosen Publishing Group, Inc.

First Edition

Cataloging-in-Publication Data

Names: Benson, Kerry E., author.
Title: Opioids / Kerry E. Benson.
Description: First Edition. | New York : Rosen Publishing, 2020 | Series: Facts and fiction about drugs | Includes bibliographical references and index. | Audience: Grades 5–8.
Identifiers: ISBN 9781725347670 (library binding) | ISBN 9781725347663 (paperback)
Subjects: LCSH: Opioid abuse—Juvenile literature. | Opioids—Juvenile literature. | Drug abuse—Juvenile literature.
Classification: LCC RC568.O45 B46 2020 | DDC 362.29'3—dc23

Some of the images in this book illustrate individuals who are models.
The depictions do not imply actual situations or events.

Manufactured in the United States of America

CONTENTS

INTRODUCTION

Prescription painkillers are powerful enough to kill severe pain—and, when they're misused, they're powerful enough to kill a person. Nobody expects to be the person whose future is destroyed by drugs. When people pop that first pill into their mouth, nobody expects that someday soon they won't be able to stop. But millions of people are battling an addiction to painkillers, and millions more will become addicted in the years to come.

"I'll just try one pill," one might say, or, "If doctors give this out to their patients, how dangerous can it be?"

Don't be fooled. In 2017, drug overdoses ranked as the number-one cause of death for Americans under the age of fifty. In other words, drugs—especially opioids, which are the most powerful kind of painkiller—had killed more people than guns, cancer, or car crashes. Sometimes, these victims died from a single pill or extra-strong injection.

On the other hand, statistics about teenage drug use show that there is hope. According to the National Institute on Drug Abuse (NIDA), only 4.2 percent of high school seniors abused prescription opioids in 2017, compared to 9.5 percent in 2004. This means most teens have chosen not to abuse pain medications.

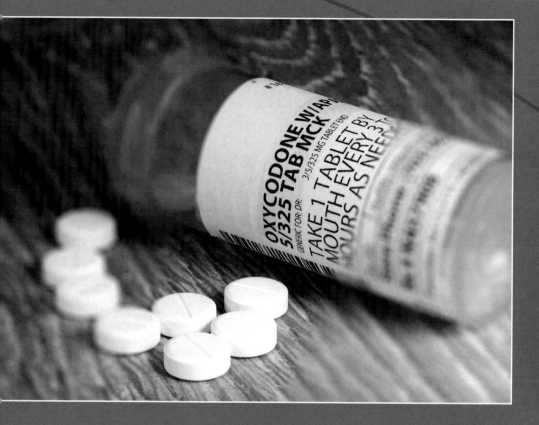

Opioids are powerful painkillers, and millions of people are addicted to them. Some people become addicted after taking them to control pain after surgery or an injury.

Many of us know someone who is struggling with opioid addiction, or maybe you're just overwhelmed by all the information out there and trying to make sense of what you're hearing. This resource will help you gain some clarity.

More Than Just Painkillers

Over 5,400 years ago, a group of people from the Middle East found some flowers with a rather strange power. These flowers, called poppies, produce a white goo called opium. When these ancient people tasted opium, they felt weirdly spaced-out. In the thousands of years after they lived, many other civilizations would discover opium, too. They quickly realized that it was a powerful painkiller.

Even today, many opioids come from the opium found in the poppy plant. These natural opioids are called opiates. They include drugs like morphine and codeine. Other opioids are synthetic. Synthetic opioids are either made completely from artificial chemicals, or they're made by adding chemicals to a natural opioid. For example, heroin is made by chemically changing morphine in a laboratory. Another synthetic opioid, fentanyl, is completely artificial and involves a very complicated

Poppies are no ordinary flowers. Part of the plant contains a natural opioid: a gooey substance called opium. Some other opioids, like morphine, can be extracted from opium.

recipe of chemicals. A drug is considered an opioid if it comes from opium or is made from chemicals to act like opium.

How Are Opioids Different from Other Painkillers?

At some point in their lives, most people have taken mild pain relievers, like Advil or Tylenol. These medicines are called over-the-counter medicines. "Over-the-counter" means that a person can buy them from a pharmacy without a doctor's prescription.

Some painkillers can only be prescribed by a doctor after an office visit. Most prescription painkillers are opioids.

These medicines can be unsafe if someone takes too much or uses them incorrectly. However, they aren't nearly as risky as prescription painkillers.

Prescription painkillers are stronger than over-the-counter painkillers. Because of this, a doctor must write a prescription to allow patients to get them from a pharmacy. Most prescription painkillers are opioids. However, you won't find all opioids at a pharmacy. Some opioids, like heroin, are illegal.

Opioids can be really helpful in some situations. If your doctor prescribes you opioids, there's no reason to be afraid. Just be very careful, and be sure to follow your doctor's instructions. Many people become addicted to opioids after a doctor prescribes pain pills for them.

WILL POPPY SEED BAGELS GET ME HIGH?

No ... but they can cause people to fail a drug test! Poppy seeds—those tiny black seeds found in muffins and on bagels—contain a small amount of opioids. They don't have enough to make a person feel drugged, but they may be enough to accidentally turn a drug test positive. Drug tests can't tell the difference between the opioids in poppy seeds and opioid drugs, and the opioids from poppy seeds can remain in the body for several days. Moral of the story: if you're asked to take a drug test, beware of poppy seeds!

Endorphins: The Opioids Inside You

Even people who have never taken an opioid drug have experienced the effects of opioids. That's because the body makes and releases its own natural opioids: feel-good chemicals called endorphins! Endorphins make people happy. For example, some people say they get a runner's high, which is a feeling of pleasure after exercise. It's widely believed that this "high" happens because exercise causes endorphins to be released. Some research points to other triggers, too. To experience a rush of endorphins, you might also try meditating, laughing, eating chocolate, or munching on a chili pepper!

Opioid drugs are chemically similar to endorphins. Just like endorphins, these drugs attach to a special spot in the brain to block pain signals. In fact, opioid drugs work by tricking the body into thinking that they're endorphins. But make no mistake: while endorphins are safe, opioid drugs can be dangerous. For starters,

The body makes and releases natural opioids called endorphins. Endorphins make people feel good, and, unlike opioid drugs, they are not addictive. Activities like running can trigger their release.

opioid drugs are much stronger than the body's endorphins. Also, opioid drugs are much more addictive. Almost immediately after endorphins attach to the brain, the body breaks them down. On the other hand, it's much harder for the body to break down opioid drugs. Therefore, these drugs stick around for longer and can cause problems.

The Other Opioids

Opioid drugs can be made in two ways: they're either made from opium in the poppy plant, or they're created in a lab to act like opium.

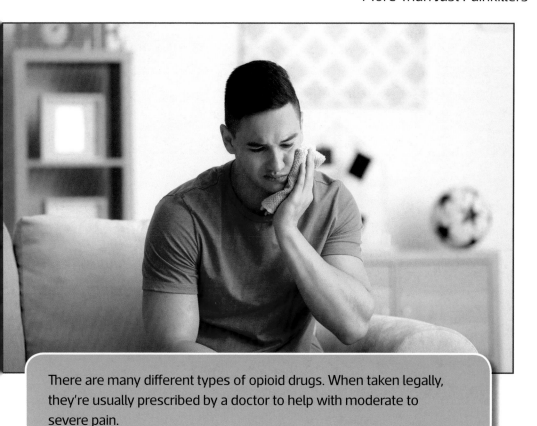

There are many different types of opioid drugs. When taken legally, they're usually prescribed by a doctor to help with moderate to severe pain.

Codeine and morphine are opioids that scientists can extract directly from opium. Morphine is about ten times stronger than opium, so doctors will prescribe it only to treat severe pain. Codeine, on the other hand, is used for mild or moderate pain. This drug is one of the most commonly used opioids. It's often combined with Tylenol.

Scientists can change codeine to create an even stronger kind of opioid called hydrocodone. Hydrocodone is frequently sold under the brand name Vicodin. It is very addictive, so it's a commonly abused drug. But it's not abused as badly as oxycodone. Oxycodone (also known as OxyContin, Oxy, or Percocet) can be created from opium in a lab. This drug is taken as a pill for moderate or severe pain. When oxycodone started being sold in the United States in 1996, a lot of users became addicted to the drug.

But a particularly scary opioid called heroin is even more addictive than oxycodone. This drug was accidentally created by a scientist who was fiddling with the chemical structure of morphine. At first, researchers thought this substance was safe. In fact, in the early 1900s, people could find heroin products at their local pharmacy. They could buy heroin cough drops and even heroin medicine to make babies fall asleep! But then people began to realize how addictive and dangerous heroin is. By 1924, it became illegal in the United States. Many heroin users start their drug problem by abusing prescription pills. Then, when they run out of prescription pills, can't afford them, or want something stronger, they move on to injecting heroin. These injections are especially dangerous. Heroin is twice as strong as morphine, and it is responsible for killing thousands of Americans each year.

Part of the reason heroin is so dangerous is because illegal-drug dealers sometimes mix it with an even more powerful opioid called fentanyl. Fentanyl is a drug that is made in a lab, and it's a hundred times stronger than morphine. It is incredibly powerful: even a tiny amount can be deadly. Illegal-drug users often don't even realize when fentanyl has been added to another opioid they're taking.

Most opioids are taken to relieve pain or are abused by people who are trying to get high. But some opioids are actually used to help people overcome addictions! There are two main drugs that fall into this category: methadone and buprenorphine. Methadone and buprenorphine lock into the same parts of the brain as other opioids. They work by blocking the effects of these

ATTENTION: A NOTE ABOUT ATTENTION-DEFICIT MEDICATION AND ANTIANXIETY DRUGS

Painkillers aren't the only kind of prescription medications that people abuse. Some people take other kinds of pills that aren't prescribed to them, like attention-deficit medication or antianxiety pills.

Attention-deficit pills, like Ritalin, can help people who have a hard time focusing. However, they should never be taken without a prescription. According to a 2017 study from SUNY Buffalo, these pills can hurt the brain when they're taken by someone who doesn't have attention-deficit disorder. As a result, they may cause problems with behavior and sleep.

Unprescribed antianxiety pills can also be dangerous. These drugs make the brain work more slowly, so they can make users feel very tired, confused, and dizzy. If people take too many of these pills at once, they may even have trouble breathing.

other opioids. However, methadone and buprenorphine don't work for every addicted person. Sometimes, drug users develop an addiction to these drugs, too.

Checking the Fine Print: What Are the Side Effects?

Whether people are using opioids to control pain or abusing them to get high, they'll usually experience some side effects. Side effects are additional effects that are separate from the main purpose of a drug. For example, the main purpose of opioids is to reduce pain. However, they may also cause some unpleasant effects. These effects include nausea, dizziness, constipation, and tiredness. Furthermore, at doses that are too high, opioids can slow down breathing and be deadly. This risk increases when people use opioids with other substances that also slow down breathing, like alcohol or sleeping pills.

Despite this danger, side effects are a fairly small problem for most people. Many patients take opioids only for a short time, and once they stop, those side effects disappear. For people battling an opioid problem, the bigger struggle usually begins later ... when they realize they can't stop.

CHAPTER TWO

The Power of Addiction

Just like a hacker can take over a computer, opioids can hack a person's brain. Think about it this way: When a computer gets hacked, it is under the control of the hackers. The computer will listen to whatever the hackers tell it to do, even if the hackers' commands are harmful. People who become addicted to opioids lose control, too. Their brain constantly tells them to use opioids. They can't stop thinking about how to get another dose, and they often feel like it's impossible to quit.

Addiction doesn't mean that a person is bad or weak. Sure, in most cases, an addicted person is at least partly responsible for her situation: after all, everyone makes decisions about whether to use drugs. But an addicted person cannot control how her body and brain will react to drugs. Because every person's body is different, it's easier for some people to develop addictions than others. Many times, addiction runs in families. Children

People who develop dependence on a drug feel sick if they try to stop taking it. Many people who have experienced dependence say stopping taking the drug makes them feel like they have the flu.

of addicted parents are often more likely to become addicts themselves, for example. Addiction also changes the way the brain works. For these reasons, many researchers believe that addiction should be treated as a disease, just like cancer or diabetes.

When thinking about addiction, it's helpful to understand the difference between three key terms: tolerance, dependence, and addiction. Tolerance means that a person's body learns to react less to a drug over time. As the body gets used to the drug, the drug user needs to take more and more of it in order to feel the same effects. Dependence means that the body starts to rely on the drug. Because of this, a drug-dependent person will feel physically sick if he tries to stop taking it. Lastly, addiction is an uncontrollable, overwhelming need to use a drug. These three situations can happen separately. A person can develop tolerance to a drug without being addicted or dependent on it, for example. Or he can become dependent without having an addiction. But they often happen together.

The Dangers of Tolerance

Usually, people think of tolerance as something good. Tolerating differences is important, and if someone tolerates her little brother's nonstop questions, she is patient. But drug tolerance—the body's tendency to react less to a drug over time—is often bad.

Sometimes tolerance is just plain frustrating. At first, a person might need only two pain-relieving pills to dull the pain of an injury, for example. But in time, that same person might need three pills to get rid of the same amount of pain. In other words, the pills became less effective as the body got used to the drug.

Other times, tolerance can be dangerous. Imagine this: A drug addict usually does drugs in her bedroom. Every day, she injects herself with a large dose of drugs while sitting on her bedroom floor. But one day, instead of doing drugs in her bedroom, she goes to a friend's house. She injects the same dose as the day before—but this time, she's sitting in her friend's kitchen. Immediately after the injection, she stops breathing.

What changed? She took the same amount of the drug as she usually did … but now, it's deadly. This is an example of a specific kind of tolerance called environmental tolerance. Environmental tolerance happens when the body gets used to taking a drug in a certain place and becomes tolerant to its effects only in that place.

Drugs can be especially dangerous if people suddenly take them in a new location. Because of environmental tolerance, the body adjusts to a drug only in one specific place.

Why does environmental tolerance happen? Well, when a person uses a drug, her brain isn't just focusing on that drug. Her brain also takes in the details of her surroundings, like the color of the walls, the scent of the air, and the objects around her. If she does a drug in the same room every time, her brain eventually learns to prepare itself for the drug whenever she's in that room. Her bedroom's green walls and wooden dresser might remind her brain, "Get ready. The drug is coming." But when she suddenly uses the same dose of drug somewhere new, her brain is caught off guard. Her body doesn't expect the drug to come, so it doesn't prepare, and the "usual" dose becomes extra risky.

And here's another reason why tolerance can be dangerous: most drugs affect the body in more than one way, but people do not always become tolerant to all of those effects equally. For example, people often quickly become tolerant to the high they get from opioids. That means they require more and more of the drug in order to feel high. However, they may not have developed tolerance to a different effect of the drug: slowed breathing. This means that as they increase their dose to try to get high again, they may stop breathing.

Dependence: Shouting in a Silent Stadium

Think of a time when you were really sick—not just with a common cold, but with an illness like the flu. Do you remember how that felt? Maybe you were throwing up, and your body felt weak and achy, and you were shaking, sweaty, and feverish. That's usually what it feels like when people try to stop taking an opioid they're dependent on.

Dependence happens because the brain adjusts to the presence of opioids. Normally, the brain sends out chemicals to keep a person awake, alert, and breathing steadily. When opioids attach to the brain, they stop the brain from releasing as many of these chemicals. That's why opioids can cause tiredness and slower breathing. Eventually, though, the brain learns to increase the amount of chemicals it sends out. That way, even when opioids stop some of those chemicals, a person still has a "normal" amount of chemicals in the body. But then, if a person suddenly stops taking opioids, the brain doesn't have time to adjust: it still sends out the extra chemicals. Now, there's a ton of those chemicals in the body and no opioids to stop some of them from being released. In large amounts, these chemicals make a person feel sick. These sick feelings are called withdrawal.

Have you ever been at a sports game, having a conversation with a normal speaking voice ... and suddenly, the crowd roars and you have to shout to be heard? Then imagine the stadium goes silent in the middle of your sentence. You're still shouting, but now your voice seems earsplittingly loud. That's what dependence is like: The body learns to "shout"—to send out extra chemicals to make up for opioids. When the opioids suddenly disappear, the body doesn't have time to readjust. Just like a person who speaks loudly in a silent stadium, the body keeps sending out extra chemicals, even when it doesn't have to anymore.

Addiction: Why Can't People Just Stop?

Dependence happens when opioids take over your body, but addiction happens when opioids take over your life. People who are addicted to opioids usually battle the physical symptoms of dependence, too. That means they'll feel like they have the flu if they try to stop taking the drug. But they also feel the psychological symptoms of addiction. They won't be able to stop thinking about the drug, and they'll feel an overwhelming urge to keep taking it ... even if they realize that it's ruining their life.

Addiction cravings are like hunger: If you stop eating for a couple of days, you'll be so hungry that you won't be able to stop thinking about food. You can't "turn off" your feelings of hunger, just as an addicted person can't turn off cravings for a drug. If you haven't eaten for several days and someone offers you a

WHAT'S IN A NAME?

The word "addiction" comes from ancient Rome, and it originally had nothing to do with drugs or alcohol. Thousands of years ago, an "addictus" was a person who was forced by a judge to become someone else's slave. This "addictus" was usually someone who owed money to another person and wasn't paying it back. People didn't start using the word "addiction" to talk about an uncontrollable need to use drugs until the 1900s. But it makes sense why they did: for people who struggle with drug addiction, it's almost as if they're a slave to drugs. Drugs control an addict's life, just as a slave master once controlled an addictus's life.

slice of cake, it will be really difficult—almost impossible—to resist. Our bodies are naturally wired to crave food, and people who battle opioid addiction also become wired to crave opioids.

Breaking the Cycle of Addiction

Overcoming opioid addiction is challenging. According to the National Institute on Drug Abuse (NIDA), between 40 and 60 percent of people with drug addiction problems will relapse. This means they go back to using drugs again. But luckily, certain treatments can improve people's chances of ending a drug habit forever.

Some people who are addicted to opioids try to stop taking drugs all at once. But this is often an unsuccessful strategy because people who are addicted often feel really sick when they suddenly stop taking opioids. Hoping to feel better, they then begin using drugs again. Therefore, many treatment

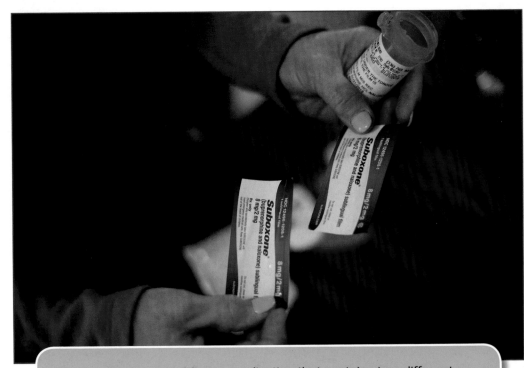

Suboxone is an antiaddiction medication that contains two different drugs: buprenorphine and naloxone. This drug combination can help people overcome an addiction to opioids.

centers recommend tackling addiction with a combination of medication and counseling. The two main medications used to fight addiction are called methadone and buprenorphine.

One reason why methadone and buprenorphine are helpful is that they fight withdrawal symptoms. This means that people taking one of these drugs don't feel as sick when they try to stop taking the opioid they're addicted to.

These drugs also work to make other opioids less effective. Methadone and buprenorphine attach to the same area of the brain as other opioids, but they attach more firmly. Therefore, if someone takes buprenorphine and then tries to use another opioid, like heroin, the heroin won't be able to attach to the brain as easily. Buprenorphine will have already attached to the places that heroin tries to occupy. As a result, the person won't feel the usual high from heroin.

Methadone and buprenorphine are both opioids, but they aren't as dangerous as other kinds of opioids, like heroin. They still aren't risk free, though. Because they're opioids, some people end up abusing methadone or buprenorphine, too.

With this in mind, many addiction treatment centers prescribe a medicine that contains both buprenorphine and another drug called naloxone. Naloxone is a drug that blocks opioids from attaching to the brain. However, unlike buprenorphine, it's not an opioid. If people try to abuse opioids while they take this buprenorphine-naloxone drug, the naloxone in the drug will make them feel sick. Naloxone doesn't just help people fight addiction, though. If somebody overdoses on opioids, a naloxone injection can sometimes reverse that overdose. This injection may be very unpleasant and painful because it causes instant, severe withdrawal— but it can save lives.

Reducing Your Risk

Maybe you've heard the expression "Prevention is better than cure." This is a fancy way of saying that it is better to stop something bad from happening than to try to fix it after it has happened. It definitely applies to drug addiction: it is much easier never to become addicted to drugs at all than it is to end an addiction after it has started.

Nobody tries to develop an addiction to drugs. People often don't even realize that they're addicted until it's too late. But a little knowledge and caution can go a long way toward preventing addiction.

From Prescription to Addiction

Addicted people's first encounter with opioids isn't always at a party or in a dark alley on the streets. For many people, it's actually at a doctor's office. If someone has a ski accident, for example, a doctor might prescribe opioids for the pain. At first, the pills seem to work great, but as the patient takes more and more, he notices something strange: he feels like he needs them to get through his day. To make matters worse, as his body gets used to the pills, they aren't working as well as they used to. Instead of taking just one pill to numb the pain, he needs three pills to get the same effect. His ski injuries have healed, but his body has become addicted to painkillers. He now feels sick if he skips a dose. When his prescription runs out, he steals pain pills from other people or spends lots of money to buy pills illegally. He's desperate to feel normal again.

That scenario doesn't always happen, of course. Plenty of people who are prescribed opioids by their doctor do not get addicted. But it's important for them to be careful with their prescriptions to avoid falling into that trap.

To prevent addiction, patients should follow their doctor's instructions carefully. They should never take more than the recommended dose without a doctor's permission. In addition, they should try not to take more medication than necessary. For example, if they still feel pretty good when it's time for their next dose, they should consider waiting before taking another pill.

In certain situations, nonopioid pain medications can work just as well as opioids to control pain and without as many side effects. But sometimes opioids are the best option immediately after surgery or an injury. If that's the case, patients should ask their doctors when they're allowed to switch to over-the-counter painkillers.

Patients should also be aware that they don't have to finish their prescription. If a doctor prescribes twenty pain pills, but the patient used only six and doesn't need more, he should stop taking them.

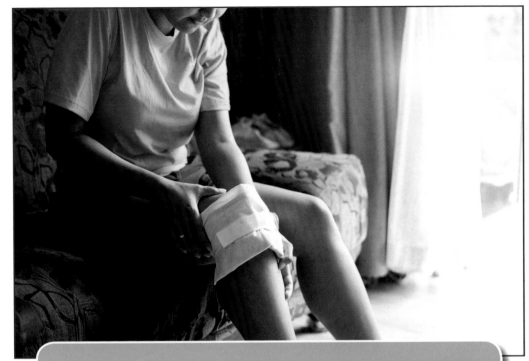

Medication isn't the only way to reduce pain. Other strategies, like icing, applying heat, distraction, or even drinking cherry juice, may help people find relief.

Lastly, patients can check with their doctor about other pain management strategies. They might be able to get more comfortable by heating or icing their injuries or distracting themselves with movies. Drinking cherry juice may also help; cherries contain a natural pain reliever!

Tempted to Say Yes?

Even when they know that drugs can cause big problems, some teens are tempted to give them a try. There are many reasons why people might decide to misuse opioids, but saying no is the smarter choice.

DOS AND DON'TS

DO read reputable websites, articles, and books about drugs.
DON'T trust information from somebody who's trying to sell you drugs. Drug dealers often lie about how dangerous or addictive a drug is because they're trying to sell to as many people as possible.

DO check with a doctor before using any prescription drugs. Even if a pill is safe for one person, someone else's body may react differently.
DON'T just believe that a pill is safe. Pills that people buy illegally are not held to the same safety standards as pills from a pharmacy. Many people have died after taking pills that were accidentally made too strong.

DO check your internet sources! Especially if it's a Wikipedia article, blog site, or forum, the information may be inaccurate. Anybody can edit a Wikipedia page, start a blog, or comment on a forum.
DON'T believe everything you read on the internet about drugs.

Sometimes, teenagers assume everyone is taking pills and they want to fit in. The fact is most people (teens included) don't misuse pills. According to information from NIDA, only 4.2 percent of high school seniors misused opioids in 2017. This means that about ninety-six out of every one hundred high school seniors did not misuse opioids.

Others may turn to pills because they're suffering from physical pain. Opioids prescribed by a doctor can help with this, especially if the pain is temporary. But they often cause more problems than they solve. Even in nonaddicted people, opioids can cause a bunch of unpleasant side effects. Furthermore, people who become addicted to opioids usually feel sick if they try to stop taking the drug. They may also feel pain more strongly than before their addiction.

Some people may think that drugs will help them feel better when they're stressed, bored, or upset. It's understandable to wish for a quick, easy solution to escape difficult feelings. However, pain pills are not the solution. People who are addicted often say they would do anything to go back in time and undo their choice to try drugs. They don't have that choice anymore—but

Some teens might be tempted to try drugs when they're feeling stressed or bored. Instead, try a new activity, such as photography. The possibilities are endless!

other people do. Teens who are considering drugs can choose to fight back against a moment of curiosity and turn toward other activities that will help them cope with life's challenges. They might decide to write in a journal, watch a movie with a friend, or try a new hobby like rock climbing or photography. Every person has options and potential; they shouldn't give drugs the chance to steal their future.

How to Say No

Maybe you've heard that if someone offers you drugs, you should "just say no." True, you *should* say no, but sometimes it's not that easy. Thinking of some strategies in advance and considering which ones feel most comfortable for you will make it easier to refuse drugs if somebody tries to give them to you. If a simple "no thanks" doesn't do the trick, here are some other suggestions:

"No way—if my parents found out, I'd be in so much trouble!"

"I'll pass. If my coach found out, I'd get kicked off the baseball team."

"No thanks, I have a [friend, uncle, cousin, etc.] who got into drugs, and they wrecked his life."

"That's not really my thing."

Or just move on to something else. Walk away, pretend to be busy texting a friend, or mention that there's somewhere else you have to be. In a situation like this, it's OK to make up excuses that may not be true—you're protecting your future.

Above all, your body is yours and yours alone, and nobody has the right to tell you what to do with it. Remember, just

If you plan ahead and think about what strategies feel most comfortable to you, it will be easier to refuse drugs when someone tries to offer them to you.

as you have the right to expect respect from others, you owe that respect to yourself. You only get one body; honor it and treat it well.

Is Addiction in Your Blood?

Genetics, or genes, give the body and brain instructions about how to develop and function. Genes are the reason why curly hair, green eyes, or tiny feet often run in families. Scientists have even discovered genes that explain why cilantro tastes soapy to some people but not to others! And, as it turns out, genes are partly to blame for addiction.

Many different genes seem to be involved in addiction. For example, there may be certain genes that make people more likely to start using drugs. Other genes may determine how a person feels when taking a drug. Genetics also help explain why it's so hard for some people to stop drug use once they've started. People whose relatives have battled addiction should be extra careful around addictive substances. Because addiction runs in families, these people may be more likely to develop an addiction themselves.

Does this mean that someone is doomed to a life of addiction if she has an addicted parent, sibling, or other relative? Not at all. A person's choices, values, attitudes, and environment are also important factors. Someone with a strong family history of drug abuse who decides never to touch opioids will never become addicted to them. Likewise, even a person without any family history of addiction can become a victim of drugs. It takes only one bad decision.

Finding and
oviding Suppo

ou have family members or friends who are addicted
, the first thing you should know is that it's not your f
ey're addicted, and it's not your fault if they can't s
n't have control over someone else's drug problem.
to find control in other areas of your life and to ider
s of support. You aren't alone.

Having a friend or family member who struggles with
addiction can be really hard. Here are some strategies
to help you cope.

Make a list of people you trust whom you can contact
n an emergency. Keep their phone numbers in a safe
place. The list could include neighbors, close family
friends, teachers, trusted relatives, and crisis hotlines
f you're worried about your safety, agree upon a "safe
word" with some of those trusted people. A safe word
s just one unusual word or phrase you could say to
signal that you're feeling unsafe and need help. This

In case of emergency, save the numbers of people you trust. Store these numbers somewhere safe, and if you have your own phone, add them to your contacts list.

is especially helpful if you're worried that you'll "freeze up" in an emergency situation or if you just don't feel like explaining everything that's going on.

- Make a list of safe places you could go to if you needed to get away for a few hours or possibly even overnight. Safe places could include the library, a friend or family member's house, the gym, a teen center, place of worship, or park. You can turn to these places even if there's no emergency; when home life is stressful, sometimes it helps to have an escape. Just make sure to tell your family where you're going.

- Keep a journal; sometimes it helps to have somewhere to let your feelings out when you don't feel like talking. If you're afraid someone will find what you've written, it's OK to use code words or

change people's names.
- Dedicate yourself to a hobby. Art, music, writing, or a favorite sport can help release difficult feelings.
- If your family member or friend is away at a treatment clinic or you cannot visit for another reason and it's safe to stay in touch, consider writing this person letters. These letters don't have to be anything deep. Don't feel pressured to talk about addiction or recovery if you don't want to. But just writing to this person could help encourage both of you.

Know the Signs

It's not always easy to tell if someone is struggling with an opioid addiction. However, there are certain clues to keep an eye out for. People who are taking opioids often act tired, especially when they first start their habit. Their pupils will often be very small. They might not be as clean or as neat as usual, and they may complain of feeling sick to their stomach.

Oftentimes, people who start using drugs will skip school or work, and their behavior will change. They might act sad, angry, or nervous, and they might not hang out with friends as much as they used to. If they're injecting drugs, they might try to hide the needle marks by wearing long-sleeved shirts even when it's hot outside.

Of course, these signs don't always mean that someone is using drugs. Someone could be tired from staying up late. If your brother complains of nausea, he might just have a stomach bug. Someone who acts upset could be dealing with family problems or a mental health issue like anxiety or depression. And maybe a friend who wears long-sleeved shirts all the time simply gets cold easily. But if several of these signs occur together, and

RELIABLE RESOURCES

If someone you know is struggling with addiction and you need help or information, you have many options. You can talk to a teacher, guidance counselor, or other trusted authority figure, or you can try these resources:

- **Nar-Anon:** http://www.nar-anon.com: A free support group for families and close friends of people who struggle (or have struggled) with drug addiction; some states even have a support group especially for teens, called Narateen.
- **Crisis Text Line:** Text HOME to 741741 anywhere in the United States: offers free, 24/7 text support for anyone dealing with a difficult situation.
- **SAMHSA's National Helpline:** 1-800-662-HELP (4357): A free and confidential phone number to call for advice about drug-related treatment/support for yourself or someone you know, and it's available in both English and Spanish.
- **American Addiction Centers Guide for Children of Addicted Parents:** https://americanaddictioncenters .org/guide-for-children: This page describes the difficulties kids may experience when parents are addicted or going through treatment, and it offers advice and further resources for getting help.

you get a feeling that something might not be right, don't take chances. Tell an adult you trust. You might just save a life.

Also keep an eye out for other signs of drug use, like missing prescription medications and empty pill bottles. Missing money or valuable items could be a sign, too. Sometimes, people with drug addictions steal from their friends and family because they're so desperate to buy drugs. They know that stealing isn't right, and they don't want to take from you. But when addiction sets in, it controls a person's life.

Building a Better Future

If someone close to you uses drugs, getting help can be scary or shameful. You might be afraid of getting your friend or family member in trouble or worried about what other people will think.

Sometimes, teens are reluctant to reach out for help when someone they know is using drugs. But reaching out is important, and it's nothing to be ashamed of.

But safety is the number-one concern, and there's no reason to be ashamed. Opioid addiction is a condition that a lot of people battle; many of us know someone who has struggled with it. A 2018 survey conducted by the American Psychiatric Association found that 31 percent of Americans know somebody who is (or was) addicted to opioids.

It's also important to think about how difficult circumstances can be used to shape your future in a positive way. If someone you care deeply about is addicted, you probably understand the pain of addiction firsthand. Honor this person's struggle with a promise to bring something positive out of the brokenness you have witnessed: Tell yourself you will never misuse drugs. Then, keep that commitment for as long as you live. In fact, you should commit to this even if you don't know anybody who has struggled with opioids. You may not be able to protect other people's futures from addiction—but you can protect your own.

ADDICTION An uncontrollable, overwhelming need to use a drug.

BUPRENORPHINE An opioid drug that is often used to help people overcome drug addiction by stopping other opioids from attaching to the brain.

DEPENDENCE A situation in which the body starts to rely on a drug. Stopping the drug causes a person to feel physically ill.

ENDORPHINS Opioid chemicals that the body makes and releases on its own. These chemicals attach to the same place in the brain as opioid drugs.

FENTANYL An extremely powerful opioid drug that is created in a laboratory.

GENE A small unit of information in the body that helps determine each person's characteristics, like hair color, eye color, and height. Genes also play a role in determining how easily somebody develops addiction problems.

HEROIN An illegal and extremely addictive opioid drug that is similar to morphine but more powerful.

HIGH A spaced-out or happy feeling that drug users hope to get when they use drugs.

MORPHINE A powerful opioid drug that can be used for moderate or severe pain.

NALOXONE A nonopioid drug that blocks opioids from attaching to the brain. Naloxone is used in emergencies to try to reverse opioid overdoses, and it can also be added to buprenorphine to help people overcome opioid addiction.

OPIATE An opioid drug that comes naturally from the opium found in the poppy plant. Opiate drugs include morphine and codeine.

OPIOID A substance—usually a drug—that attaches to a specific place in the brain and turns on this brain area. These substances help relieve pain, but opioid drugs can be very dangerous and addictive.

OPIUM An opioid that comes from the sticky, white goo in the poppy plant. Other opioid drugs either come from opium or are made to act similarly to opium.

OVERDOSE To take more of a drug than the body can handle.

OVER-THE-COUNTER PAINKILLER A pain-relieving drug that a person can buy from the pharmacy without a doctor's prescription.

OXYCODONE A powerful, addictive opioid that can be used to treat moderate or severe pain. This drug is sometimes called by the brand names OxyContin or Percocet.

PRESCRIPTION PAINKILLER A pain-relieving drug that a person can get only from a pharmacy if a doctor writes a prescription.

PUPIL The black spot in the center of a person's eye that allows light in. When somebody takes opioid drugs, sometimes this black spot looks smaller than usual.

RELAPSE To go back to using drugs after trying to stop an addiction.

SIDE EFFECT An additional effect that is separate from the main effect a person is trying to get from a drug.

SYNTHETIC Not natural. Synthetic opioids are either made completely from artificial chemicals, or they're made by adding chemicals to a natural opioid.

TOLERANCE The body's tendency to react less to a drug over time.

WITHDRAWAL The sick, often flu-like feelings a person experiences after stopping a drug the body has become dependent on.

Crisis Text Line
Text: text HOME to 741741 (in US)
Website: https://www.crisistextline.org
Facebook, Twitter, and Instagram: @crisistextline
Crisis Text Line offers free, 24/7 support for people in the United States who need help dealing with a difficult situation or painful emotion.

Drug Free Kids Canada
PO Box 23013
Toronto, ON M5N 3A8
Canada
(416) 479-6972
Website: https://www.drugfreekidscanada.org
Facebook: @DrugFreeKidsCanada
Twitter: @DrugFreeKidsCda
This charity aims to raise awareness about substance use in order to reduce addiction in young people.

Foundation for a Drug-Free World
6331 Hollywood Boulevard
Los Angeles, CA 90028
Website: https://www.drugfreeworld.org
Facebook: @DFWInt
Twitter: @drugfreeworld
This nonprofit is dedicated to producing engaging educational materials that teach the public about the dangers of drug use.

Kids Help Phone (Canada)
1-800-668-6868
Live Chat: https://kidshelpphone.ca/live-chat
Text: text CONNECT to 686868
Website: https://kidshelpphone.ca
Facebook, Twitter, and Instagram: @KidsHelpPhone
This charity offers a free, confidential, 24/7 telephone service
   for young people in Canada who are struggling with any
   problem and need somebody to listen. This service is
   available in both English and French, and counselors can
   also connect with kids through live chat and text.

Narcotics Anonymous (Nar-Anon)
23110 Crenshaw Boulevard, Suite A
Torrance, CA 90505
(800) 477-6291
Website: https://www.nar-anon.org
Nar-Anon for Teens: https://www.nar-anon.org/narateen
Email: wso@nar-anon.org (English) and osm@nar-anon.org
   (Spanish)
Nar-Anon is a free support group for family members and close
   friends of people who struggle (or have struggled) with drug
   addiction. Local group meetings take place in communities
   across the United States and Canada. Some communities
   also have Nar-Anon groups specifically for teens,
   called Narateen.

Natural High
7881-A Drury Lane
La Jolla, CA 92037
(858) 551-7006

Website: https://naturalhigh.org
Email: info@naturalhigh.org
Facebook and Instagram: @livenaturallyhigh
Twitter: @NaturalHigh
 Natural High encourages people to turn to activities that uplift
    and inspire them instead of using alcohol or drugs.

Partnership for Drug-Free Kids and Center on Addiction
633 Third Avenue, 19th Floor
New York, NY 10011-6706
(212) 922-1560
Website: https://drugfree.org
Facebook: @partnershipdrugfree
Instagram and Twitter: @thepartnership
These two nonprofits aim to change how the nation talks about
    addiction through drug prevention programs and by
    supporting families struggling with addiction.

Shatterproof
135 West 41st Street, 6th Floor
New York, NY 10036
Website: https://www.shatterproof.org
Email: info@shatterproof.org
Facebook and Twitter: @ShatterproofHQ
Instagram: @weareshatterproof
Shatterproof is a nonprofit organization dedicated to tackling
    the devastation of drug addiction. This organization works
    to support families affected by addiction, pass laws related
    to substance abuse, and increase people's understanding
    of addiction.

Bryan, Bethany. *Overcoming Addiction: Heroin, Opioid, and Painkiller Abuse*. New York, NY: Rosen Publishing, 2018.

Greek, Joe. *Coping with Opioid Abuse*. New York, NY: Rosen Publishing, 2017.

Hamilton, Tracy Brown. *Teen Life 411: I Am Addicted to Drugs: Now What?* New York, NY: Rosen Publishing, 2017.

Happe, Laura E., and Bryan Nigh. *If You Give an Ox an Oxy*. New York, NY: Morgan James Publishing, 2019.

Kenney, Karen Latchana. *Undercover Story: The Hidden Story of Drugs*. New York, NY: Rosen Publishing, 2014.

Krosoczka, Jarrett J. *Hey, Kiddo: How I Lost My Mother, Found My Father, and Dealt with Family Addiction*. New York, NY: Graphix, 2018.

Landau, Jennifer, ed. *Teens Talk About Drugs and Alcohol*. New York, NY: Rosen Publishing, 2018.

McKenzie, Precious. *How Can I Help? Friends Helping Friends: Helping a Friend with a Drug Problem*. New York, NY: Rosen Publishing, 2017.

New York Times Editorial Staff. *The Opioid Epidemic: Tracking a Crisis*. New York, NY: Rosen Publishing, 2019.

Sheff, David, and Nic Sheff. *High: Everything You Want to Know About Drugs, Alcohol, and Addiction*. New York, NY: Houghton Mifflin Harcourt, 2019.

American Addiction Centers. "Guide for Children of Addicted Parents." October 11, 2018. https://americanaddictioncenters.org/guide-for-children.

American Psychiatric Association. "APA Public Opinion Poll—Annual Meeting 2018." Newsroom, March 23–25, 2018. https://www.psychiatry.org/newsroom.apa-public-opinion-poll-annual-meeting-2018.

Crocq, Marc-Antoine. "Historical and Cultural Aspects of Man's Relationship with Addictive Drugs." *Dialogues Clin Neurosci.* 9, no. 4 (2007): 355–61.

History.com Editors. "Heroin, Morphine and Opiates." A&E Television Networks, August 21, 2018. https://www.history.com/topics/crime/history-of-heroin-morphine-and-opiates.

Kosten, Thomas R., and Tony P. George. "The Neurobiology of Opioid Dependence: Implications for Treatment." *Sci Pract. Perspect.* 1, no. 1 (2002): 13–20.

Lopresti, Courtney. "Environmental Impact on Drug Overdose: When a Usual Dose Provokes Unusual Effects." Sovereign Health Group, June 9, 2015. https://www.sovhealth.com/addiction/environmental-impact-drug-overdose-usual-dose-provokes-unusual-effects.

MacLaren, Erik. "Understanding Tolerance, Dependence, and Addiction." DrugAbuse.com, November 23, 2018. https://drugabuse.com/addiction.

Macy, Beth. *Dopesick: Dealers, Doctors, and the Drug Company that Addicted America.* New York, NY: Hachette Book Group, 2018.

National Institute on Drug Abuse. "Drugs, Brains, and Behavior: The Science of Addiction." NIH, July 2018. https://www.drugabuse.gov/publications/drugs-brains -behavior-science-addiction/treatment-recovery.

National Institute on Drug Abuse. "Vaping Popular Among Teens; Opioid Misuse at Historic Lows." NIH, December 14, 2017. https://www.drugabuse.gov/news-events/news -releases/2017/12/vaping-popular-among-teens-opioid -misuse-historic-lows.

Opiate Addiction and Treatment Resource. "Types of Opioids." September 23, 2018. http://www.opiateaddictionresource .com/opiates/types_of_opioids.

Partnership for Drug-Free Kids. "Heroin, Fentanyl, & Other Opioids." Medicine Abuse Project, 2018. https://drugfree .org.

Scheve, Tom. "What Are Endorphins?" HowStuffWorks, June 22, 2009. https://science.howstuffworks.com/life/inside -the-mind/emotions/endorphins.htm.

Thomson, Julie R. "Yes, Poppy Seeds Contain Opiates, and Here's What You Need to Know." HuffPost Taste, July 26, 2017. https://www.huffpost.com/entry/opium-poppy-seeds _n_59709d98e4b0110cb3cc64ae.

University of Utah. "Genes and Addiction." Genetic Science Learning Center, August 30, 2013. https://learn.genetics .utah.edu/content/addiction/genes.

Wilde, Cathy. "Nonprescription Use of Ritalin Linked to Adverse Side Effects, UB Study Finds." SUNY Buffalo, May 15, 2017. http://www.buffalo.edu/news /releases/2017/05/007.html.

INDEX

A

addiction
battling, 4, 5
breaking the cycle of,
  21–23, 24
changes in the brain, 16, 21
difference between tolerance
  and dependence, 16, 17
etymology of word, 21
helping people overcome, 12,
  21–22, 23, 32, 34, 37
to methadone, 13
preventing, 24, 25, 37
psychological symptoms of, 20
resources for those struggling
  with, 35
as a result of prescription
  painkillers, 8, 24–26
running in families, 15,
  30–31
sign of, 34–36
treated as a disease, 16
what it means, 15, 17,
  20–21, 36

B

brain, effect of opioids on, 9,
  12, 15, 18, 19
and addiction, 16
and endorphins, 10
and genes, 30
and methadone and
  buprenorphine, 22–23
naloxone and, 23
buprenorphine, 12, 13,
  22–23

C

codeine, 6, 11

D

dependence, 16–17, 19–20

E

endorphins, 9–10

F

fentanyl, 6–7, 12

About the Author

Kerry Benson received her undergraduate degree from Connecticut College, where she studied neuroscience. In 2018, she received a master's degree in science writing from Johns Hopkins University. She has since written for Boston University's research publication *(BU Research)*, *Hippocampus Magazine*, and other publications, and she has published two other books with Rosen Publishing: *ADA and Your Rights at School and Work* and *Everything You Need to Know About Mindfulness.*

Photo Credits

Cover Victor Moussa/Shutterstock.com; p. 5 Steve Heap/Shutterstock.com; p. 7 Volodymyr Tverdokhlib/Shutterstock.com; p. 8 wavebreakmedia/Shutterstock.com; p. 10 Dragon Images/Shutterstock.com; p. 11 Pixel-Shot/Shutterstock.com; p. 16 Jasmin Merdan/Moment/Getty Images; p. 18 Photographee.eu/Shutterstock.com; p. 22 The Washington Post/Getty Images; p. 26 Suwannee Ngoenklan/Shutterstock.com; p. 28 Artem Varnitsin/EyeEm/Getty Images; p. 30 SpeedKingz/Shutterstock.com; p. 33 Kdonmuang/Shutterstock.com; p. 36 Flamingo_Photography/iStock/Getty Images; back cover and interior speech bubbles sumkinn/Shutterstock.com.

Design and layout: Nicole Russo-Duca; Editor: Jennifer Landau; Photo Researcher: Sherri Jackson